D0905767

Or, The Ambiguities

Distributed to the trade by
SPD / Small Press Distribution
1341 Seventh Street, Berkeley, CA 94710
spdbooks.org

Funding for this book was provided by generous grant from the
National Endowment for the Arts, the New York State Council on the
Arts, and the Department of Cultural Affairs for New York City.

UGLY DUCKLING PRESSE
232 THIRD STREET #E-303
BROOKLYN, NY 11215
UGLYDUCKLINGPRESSE.ORG

NATIONAL
ENDOWMENT
FOR THE ARTS

State of the Arts
NYSCA

PRINTED IN THE UNITED STATES OF AMERICA
FIRST EDITION | FIRST PRINTING

OR, THE AMBIGUITIES

KAREN WEISER

UDP 2015

"[I]t is not for man to follow the trail of truth too far, since by so doing he entirely loses the directing compass of his mind; for arrived at the Pole, to whose barrenness it only points, there, the needle indifferently respects all points of the horizon alike."

—Herman Melville
Pierre; or, the Ambiguities

"We ought to say a feeling of *and*, a feeling of *if*, a feeling of *but*, and a feeling of *by*, quite as readily as we say a feeling of *blue* or a feeling of *cold*.

—William James
The Principles of Psychology
Chapter IX: 'The Stream of Thought'

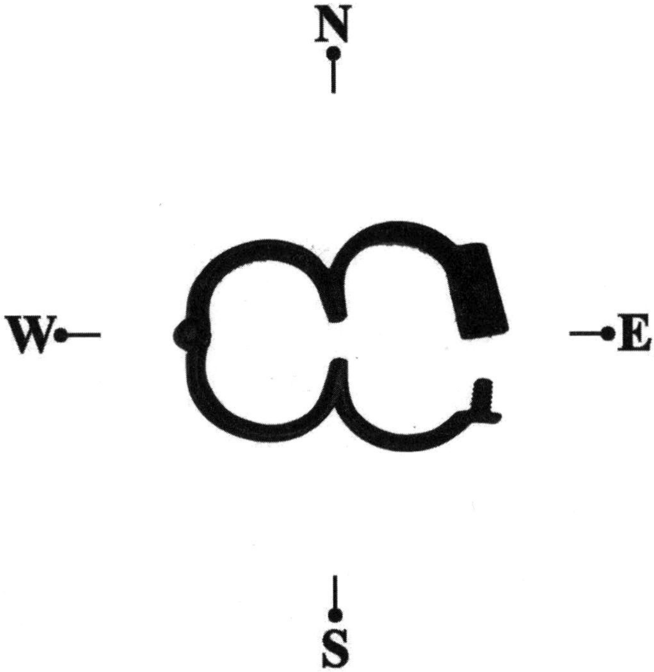
N
W
E
S

N: DEAR PIERRE

```
I was eighteen when my parents died in a plane crash. The decade after that is bare.
I  s ight   wh    y are    i  in a       rash. Th     a    t  that
I  s i t   wh      are    i  in a       sh. Th     a    t
I  s   t   h       are    i  in a       sh.
I  s       h       are    i             sh.
I  s                                    sh.
```

```
                        l o
or                      l o
or                      l o   l   s
or    he                l o   l   s   here
or    the breath        l o   l   s   here it                    b e th at      moment,
For as the breath in all our lungs is hereditary, and my present breath at this moment,
```

```
Our mirrors were covered. There were strangers in our house all day long. I don't
   ur mirror     re covered.  here    re st        s in  ur house a  day on      on
   u  mirror          over           re st        s in  u  house a       y on
   u  m           o             re st         n u     s a     y
   u  m           o             r                   s a     y
   u  m



o
o          Pier              angel
o          Pier              angel                 res t                              o
o    o Pierre,    now    angel   led            res t              and    a   liar o
out     of Pierre, but now strangely  led   th e   res t    formed, and   familiar to
outline of Pierre, but now strangely filled with features transformed, and unfamiliar to
```

```
remember eating. My clothes were torn. I wore no shoes. People only spoke to me if I
remember  at    My  othe  we   or  I  or  no sho         l  only spoke to me   I
remember         My  the        or      or   sh               only  poke   me
   ember         My  th         or                              ly   ke
   ember         My  h          o                               l    e
      be




                                                                          or
                            air                                           or              or
o                           air                            me de          or              or
o            in the  air for      m                        me dear.       or              or
no living    in the  air for   humanity,                   me dear. No more, o  no more,
no living thing in the fair form of humanity, that holds me dear. No more, oh no more,
```

spoke to them. No childhood, no home, no confirmation of memory. Symbols made me

spoke   them. No hi d   d n   me, no con ma   n   or S   ols   de m

spoke   the   o   i d   no on   a   n   or   o   de m

   ok   he   o   no   a   r   o   de

   o   he   o   no

   o

                                                                         woon

                                                         elf   swoon

           at anguish,   self   swoon.

          hat anguish,   hed   t o itself,   be   swoon.

   coil   that anguish,   had   shed him   t o itself, on the beach   his swoon.

recoil of that anguish, which had dashed him out of itself, upon the beach of his swoon.

feel again. I could feel when something was focused into a way of saying feeling. As if a

feel	in. I	feel	something	focused	a way	saying	As if
feel	I	feel	thin	used	way	in	As i
feel	I	feel	in	use	a	n	As
	I	feel		us	a	n	
	I	f					

							or
			feel			m	or
	o ear		feel			m	orph
	o ear	kin.	was	feeling		m	orph
own	no earthly	kin.	t was this feeling		oathsome,	orphan	

owned no earthly kith or kin. Yet was this feeling entirely loathsome, and orphan-like.

line was pulling me back into my body. Words gave me back a body. It was all I.
ne w s p in me back in   my   Words ave me   a body. t was all I.
ne w   p in me back in   or s ave me   o y.   s a
ne   in   in   o s a   y.   s a
ne   o s a   y.
                                     s a   y.

                                         her   e
               i   cave   her   e
— h   ow   i   cave   ther   e
—the low   river   the cave   are e ther   led   and
—the lowing river   the cave of   careless w ither be led   less   here I land
—the flowing river in the cave of man; careless whither I be led, reckless where I land

20

```
was drowned but somehow I could see a way of seeing and it has never failed me.
was    owned but     how  could   a way   see         s  ever  led me.
was    own    t    o        d   a   y                  s  ever  ed me.
was    o  n   t    o                                   s  e        e  m
    s  o           o                                   s  e        e
    s  o
```

```
"Ye      s
"Ye      s                   i
"Ye      s                   i         w        ist                        he
"Ye      s        ven    skies,    ill   w      ist                        here!
"Ye t    slaking even    skies,    ill dew and mists    til    moisture here!
"Ye thirst-slaking evening skies, ye hilly dews and mists, distil your moisture here!
```

Being still and always dead. The only wholeness a totality of change. Fourteen years later
Being till   always dead. The   whole   lit   change.   ur   n ear later
Being   always a   hole   lit   n ear later
   in   a ways a   hole   lit   later
   i   wa s   lit
   i

                                                              feel
                                         i   feel
            ere   i   feel
I f   here   peace   vi   es   to feel   f rank
I f   that there   peace   divid es   one day feel   f rank
I feel that there can be no peace in individualness. I hope one day to feel myself drank up

held her tremblingly; she bent over toward him; his mouth wet her ear; he whispered it.

```
        trembling    she bent     toward him; his        et her ear     whispered
          embling    he be                      his      et her ear     whispered
            bling    he be                                    her       w isp
             ling    be                                       her       w isp
               in                                             her       w isp
                                                                            is
```

```
I            d
I            d                         o          n          u
I    bi      d                         o          n          u  ly  re
I    bi      d      ly      nes        o          n          u  ly  re
I  ave bir   d      ly wholeness    a total        ange    l  u  ly  re
```
I gave birth and the only wholeness was a totality of change. While hugely pregnant for

Being not so much the Portal, as part of the temporary Scaffold to the Portal of this new
Being o so much the Port   a part   the temporary Scaffold   of this
Being   part   temporary   fold   or   this
Being   m   a y   this
Being   m   a y
Be

se   w
se   w   h om   e
se   w   he m s   h om   e
se   w   t   ear   laying he m s   o   h om   e
the second   we   t ear   playing he m s   host   h om   e while
the second time I went to hear a quartet playing the music Shostakovich composed while

"Whence flow the panegyrical melodies that precede the march of these heroes? From
    hence l   yrical m od es   precede the   arch of   ero s
    hence l   yric   od es   cede   arch   er s
    hence l   yric   s   a ch   e
        l   yric   s   a ch   e
                             s   a   e

        o
        o   f a   ll   s
        o   the   n   f a   ll   s   o
   move   the   n   f a i   l   sound all was   close
dying. moved the brink f a i l the sound all was close
dying. It moved me to the brink of having to leave the sound hall. I was very close

```
By vast pains we mine into the pyramid; by horrible gropings we come to the central
     vast pain          in   the pyramid;         i le      s   e    e    the centr
       st   ain              the pyramid          le       s              t   centr
            in               the pyramid;         le                      t
                             the pyr               e
                               pyr                 e



                  be                       t
     o de         be                       t
     o de         be                       t                        mir     th
     o de         be                       t           o            mir     th
     o de   then, be                       t    aught look          mir     th          reflect
  to death, then, be             pregnant.    aught look    in a mirror that       reflected
  to death, then, being nine months pregnant. Caught looking in a mirror that was reflected
```

Two books are being writ; of which the world shall only see one, and that the bungled
    book   be   writ;   which he   ll   see one, and that
    book   be   writ   he   ll   and that
    book   writ   he   ll   that
                    writ   he
                    writ

                                            in
                                        moving
           me   face   moving
      be nd me   surface   moving lose
   a mirror behind me   surfaces   moving close , push
in a mirror behind me, the surfaces of life and death moving closer, pushing in

```
thy secret I, as a seer, suspect. Grief—deep, unspeakable grief, hath made me this seer.
thy secret          suspect. Grief—d     un peak b e grief, hath          me        see
thy secret        s ect. Grief—d     un            grief, hath          me
  hy s    t                  i f                      grief, hath
                             i f                      grief
                              f                        ie



                         y        e  t
                  m      y        e  ther
   touch          m      y        e  ther
   touch    me    m      y. On  e  ther  e          rent          div  e
   touch    me,   m      aby. On the  ther side     rent          divide  my
were touching me, and my baby. On the other side of the parent and child divide, my
```

"Sir—You are a swindler. Upon the pretense of writing a popular novel for us, you have

"Sir—You are a wind   Upon the   tense   a po lar ve r s   e

     You   wind   the   tense   po lar

       o   w n   the   s   o l

       o   n   e   o

       o   n   e

    o

    o   are   o

  ions   arent   l   oving

relations   arent   l   oving

relations with my arents once   alive, moving   aught   I

relationship with my parents is once again alive, moving. The girl is my daughter and I

```
fell upon Pierre's heart, and her long hair ran over him, and arbored him in ebon
fell      Pierre      ,         long  air      h         arbor  him in ebon
 l        ie                    long  i        h         arbor  him
                                long  i        h         arbor  him
                                l                         a bor  him
                                l                         a bor


                      o             y
              t       o             my
              to      to            my
      her.    to her, to            my            was
am            her.    to her, to both o  my   what was      from
am my mother. I give to her, to both of my girls, what was taken from me.
```

S: LOVE, DELIGHT, AND ALARM

i. Preface, Part I

Along a plane I wanted to write it:
Where one end is fixed, a loose sun

To the excess of dark I was certain
That certainty's a kind of excess

A term that's but a navigating bust
A place to version a limit, feet in foot

When the lute's sum turns daily
As if by steam one could coordinate

The tulips, too numerous to pinch
By steam the autography of material

Will appear to light the vapor region
So we can know it as if by touch

A nude thing, the masses say
As they re-substantiate again

ii. Preface, Part II

What's in there to sing
Cussing its moral peepitude
Not content to festoon
Merely, but needing to festoon leaning
Against a scientific hunch
That will not apologize in this house
Of commerce, for its rupture
Or ability to suss us
Why now this impassioned youthful pause?

Mind the break

It would say—
Why this enkindled cheek and eye
With its secret prohibition
Though to speak it only makes plain
The secret's already or always
Been stolen, its pulsing voicebox
Oh tree, the face, the face
Another locus animal
Peeps down on me

iii. Pierre

I should have slept in a balloon half covered in fog
To drift together in body if not in mind
I cannot bring my mind to let go its hand
Refusing drift
Decelerate with a tug on the loom of awake
So the threads let go their pull

If I could take the middle pier into the steam
That churning thinking thing, and swallow it
As a rose turns vinyl in the sun
My distant promise of resubstantiation
A surprising eternity for a deed
Would be the ledge of dawn

At any rate I would take the middle pier
Unobliterable as the sea
Into the white shadow of a perfectly sealed box
That fails to deeply contain
One orbit of joy
A glimpse of the glorious
Subtile acid among us

iv. Pierre

Then the treehouse burned. And continued
Unobliterable as the sea
To burn. The photo of it burning

Hangs on its wall, taken from high up,
But not that high. The firemen
Approach cautiously, minus the

Four-part regimented solace, that
Would repeat. If the act of
Painting is Drawing the boundaries

Of a fire, can I disappear
Into the initial combustion? If the
Act of painting stops time or at

Least its cornet of fronted tremendous,
I could disappear into the *Encyclopedia*
of Animal Life as the cherub's sleepiest

Wet tusk. I could start with a dexterous
Periscope and end by feeling
Time, the largest block of it

I can conceive collectively:
Smell I the flowers, or thee?
See I lakes, or eyes?

v. Isabel

With its secret prohibition
The music orders my animal parts
As off a menu; said Isabel: these others

Light the vapor regions between notes
The gas-sea butter jarred into shape
Through light and its lewd manifest

So early in the morning
Between personhood and figuration
My body is not my own

A vestigial symphony none are
Meant to sound, though I am sounded
Continually, by every orbit's

Sober astronaut and her spirit freight
In the colorless shadow of a perfect
ly sealed space.

Oh tree, the face, the face
Peeps down on me

vi. Isabel

Salutations
Sister me not now
Sound the morrow against the body
Piercing certainty's kind of excess
To allay sorrow. Are you certain
Your vastation wasn't the limpid zoo
Of distress and its truest
Machination? And the ignorant
Pretend clovers? Good Morrow will steady
Us; it is our duty to steady us

We park our plovers in the white steam
To skate its cracking surface with
The simplest dream statements
From other, war-made worlds
Though they are our own
With the little we can keep in mind at once
Careless whither I be led
In mind, a memory of absent day
where I land

vii. Pierre's Father, a Ghost

Held in the palm that coin
Is a hermaphrodite vitamin, held
In the stomach, a secret palace,
And held in the ear, it's the multiplicity
Of memory unfolding
The Encyclopedia of Unfolding
Its lewdly manifest lute clarity
Interspersed with trumpeting noise
Into what kind of human shape
Will this fugue sound
An animal drift
Pulled tightly into formal expanse

With the memory of absent day all
That has come before sinks
With each unfolding
Held in the mind where it does not sound
Careless whither I be led
Reckless where I land

viii. Pierre

Held in the mind where it sounds
Some inexhaustible disruption
Art makes man an ex-lute

Scratched and skipping
Out her most-lost tune
Be equal to that claim and only equal

Inexhaustibly skipping lets in
What quierescent light
For the spectral oculus in the ear

Or the ear's proxy
I gotta sit in your seat
Or your seat's proxy to listen

To the laws of music
Please
Can I sit in your seat

This train is packed
With what quierescent light
Skips back to us

Its meadow dignified
The louder it reaches
I am all Frank

I am all unguarded

ix. Mount Greylock

This poem contains a smaller
Inner poem
Most of us know an allegory
By our own quiescent response
The echo of muted places
From the sudden shift outward
So violet in the exchange
Of motion and maintenance
Experiment and sacrament
Though no fasteners
Under day's hairnet
Hold anything still

I am somebody's landscape
At this moment exactly
Some inexhaustible disruption
Passing from one state
To another. *The Guidebook
to a Mammalian Universe*
Without its
Red opera cloak
Is often mended with
Quaint precipitation
Dashed out of oneself
Upon the beach of a swoon

x. Pierre's Mother

Oxygen-less upon the simple
August stun. A swoon collages
Time and upon it 14th century
Vienna and the baby Christ
Nay, all images are prayers
To simplify and horde senseless
Thoughts. Collapse nine months
Into a single swoon, drown—
To the castaway the beach is
Port, body, empurpled firelot
Dashed out of itself
Hosting a medical dusk
I think now
That I plainly see
It must be so

xi. Pierre

How do you say no little mystery
And mean a tinier
Unanswered memory
Limpid with precedent
By that I meant
Reason's corona
feels
Out of order
Orbs angelic
Forever unsistered

Your key, doored, is
Plainly feeling fortune
Hello fortune,
Though mutually converted, we are
Still at odds
It must be so
How do you say
love
Caustically
To make it

Feel
Like the argument it is
In the parlance
We most resemble
So I can merit my addendums
So I can confess
In unintelligible but
Delicious sounds

Sister me not, now
It must be so

xii. Pierre

Not now, noble auditor
Are your sincere transits
Ever easy

When one thing follows
It changes what it follows
And is always followed

In turn
When one thing before us
Ray gloom ray gloom ray

Is gloom
It changes what it causes
What it costs

You've lapsed with owls and virgins
Where the cumulous is without emblem
In turn

Can'st thou not cure in me this dreaminess, this
Bewilderingness I feel
A cloistered genie is quelling

In homilies but the elevator
Is not usually this
Late my poor head swims

And swims with fraternal feeling
For you, noble responder
Have become a part of this poem's

Become a part of you've become
A part of this war-
Feeling family

Was once was never but
Mysteries interpierced with mysteries, and mysteries
Roaming

Saturnalia
Before us
Responding

xiii. Isabel

Redemption narratives are twee
Rudders
In the maelstrom
Lose them though it cost a piss
Bobbling a probability bayou
With manufactured calm

So I do most carefully
Navigate between a too solid
How
And too flimsy cover
Do you say
Unmuffling footsteps

Sister me
Or the mystery
Redeems us not
Am considerate, swore
Am a wreck
With a whisper

The moving parts of hunger
Remain gravity
At the bottom of every answer
May I
um
Chorus

xiv. Narrator

Pierre,
Facts in their non-compendiums
Exile you
For a wife; and your love, a sister
Chaste
Whisper in her ear
Eight ifs to that whose minimum
Is a folio, and another if on top

Blinds you, kills you
The blankness of the
Paper, its burn
To sink a metal fig in lye
The monster dubiously
Is our affective habitat
Habit at
Minimum

xv. Pierre's Father, a Ghost

What does mind?
The portrait grates the
Solids into different shapes so
The elegy can be
From its surrounding matter
Broken to
Its simp=
Lest:

Here, not here

Said the elegy
Because I really
Meant that you love your chronometer
Into various shapes before
He opens you
Walking the voices in my head
Only
They are walking in their sleep
Into various colors
There, the needle indifferently respects all points of the horizon alike

xvi. Narrator

The elegy is a monster
Whose notes perforate your communal feeling
With its nascent consciousness
Pre-person, little tenderly
Floats this title on the fountain of philosophy
It is Doctor to the Virgo Drone
Describing completely the moment life begins
To be human
Are you acquainted with this category
Knowing little about it knowing
Nothing about the inner nature of these
Facts or what makes them what they are
Participating nonetheless
More-rificly high and temporally strident
Sweet flame of Babylon
Goes slack in a woods
Goes slack 'gainst a forceful bladder
All over the goods
Family medical history folder
No this won't decide it, not feeling pain
Not unremitting sound shapes
Nor the way one body communicates
With another in its
Continuous suede
Nut-hollow, nesting
Now it is good to believe
Dear
Pierre

E: PILGRIMAGE

Walk like somnambulists abroad,
hear humming all around
and greet it, costs nothing
but an echo hum inside.
Are you all round?

I & I'm walking but not seeing
what empty lot is walking;

I & I'm advertising greeting
in the freefall of your hum.

What is a moral compass
when the blushing throat is talking?
What is a moral judgment
when languages corrupt

This is pleasing me
enough to jail my sympathy.
My inner hum walks in woe
enough to hail my sympathy.

No pilgrimage left no more
but transits of the discrete pour

a messmate of the elements
with daedal life in boats and tents.

Precious in substance rudely wrought
habitat, which here is caught:

my paratactic hand
my buzzsaw pauses

my Angel Haze
my Observing Sky;
and here is a moment
the consequence of pivoting.

And here is my cruelty
the consequence of governing.
I & I would be improvingly
If I'd be improving

That stable proof that I would fold
into my drawer, under the lake,
into my compass, into my chart:
it is but made from other things
a music derived from vanishing

Did nearer my roses come
Did nearer my roses die

This vanishing is going low
eclipse a failing sympathy

Did nearer my planet come
Did nearer my planet go
just past where death, a legend,
follows in silence.
How may we be derived from scale?

End in a box in a hole.
End in a drawer in a lake.

This vanishing is going low—
this vanishing is going low.

W: IN THE DARBIES

            With

        these   darbies,

I'm a visual ana-   gram; my self sliced and

mirrored so I can make   sense of floating, and sink-

ing, they'll lash in hammock and drop me deep, fathoms

down, though hands in paint- ings always tell of something,

the fingers divinities, the palms bronze and held near the waist,

pointing to that which is out- side the frame, but not in your world

neither, pendant pearl from   the yard-arm end, the thing that

can't be seen but only   felt: is the hand of the artist, so

    I'll   shake   a   friendly one ere I sink,

                          b u t

                    for all that, 'tis

me, not the sen-   tence   they'll   suspend;

for at length even we feel   compelled, and that feeling

moves back to the limits of   reason, as an idea plunges

the mind into darkness; am I best when I retrace my lost origin,

or is one's legacy always inco-   herent; yes, I'm missing utilitarian

ambition and its plastering ef-   fects, which usually coincide with the

dreadfulness of this time   of year, when the sun slows the

little meager light   of thought into logic;

                                    i   t

                              tips the guard's

        cutlas and sil-   vers this nook; what other

    world can there be when   dreaming the system hangs

    it: fathoms down, fathoms   down, how I'll dream fast

    asleep, and yet waking is de-sil-   vered through these ruined

  frescoes; what other world can there be when every price melts it, a

  nature: it is dreaming that I am: fathoms down, fathoms down, for the

    likes just of me, though I've   not a friendly hand ere I sink, so

        I'll shake out my dreams,   and their spatial practice, and

              their   utopi-   an logic, ere I sink

r e -

peating   then

is   such   the

work, and such, the man

— my half-outlaw in-

junction to your self is fore-

told from the cards, though

it has long since been nearly

exhausted: Ay, Ay, Ay, all is up;

and I must go; by abandon,

though, think not of what's disclosed to the detainees but of the

alluvial bottoms of primeval regions, that are still as if unchanged

from some natural state, and I

can not get at the natural in any sense,

for it is only represented in re-

flection, though the mirror has

been de-silvered and refus-

es to show, for once, the most

comprehensible

westerly vanishing point, but

                                    here's

                              some   terrace

          in the moon   scarcely the feeling of
       earth, and once again,   for nearly the whole of the
       distance, we are alongside   the re-imagining as it bends
       toward us, witnessing, like one   bank of found objects fac-
    ing the other, tied in place with fire-hose, unnatural vines or the
    thirteenth turn of the noose, bending toward the arc of progress as
    though the world was made up   purely of letters and words, when the act
    of critique populates the loneli-   ness of our way, but then gives us only
       our own world and no pos-   sibility of another, lazily gliding
          about in the zenith,   a rapture-rendered coherence,

             as   timing   makes all labyrinths,

in the man-
their kindred, dubious
station—the trains empty
ten from the bottom of the
bottom of the sea, early in the
a final stage for a handsome sailor,
narration is apt to be less finished,
are you there?—for I do not un-
understand me, with a friendly
lashes me in hammock—

my nature and

sun-
der my starts
ifest, these ends and
like an ominous, deserted
and lights dimming—writ-
sea: this is written from the
morning, aloft from alow,
hence the conclusion of such a
with no special authority—Sentry,
derstand ambiguity, and it does not
promise to stand by the plank, it
But aren't it all sham?—since

my actions are at odds

                              heav-

                              en knows who

will have the run-   ning of me up this topical

range of reference, this cor- responding kind of thought,

for hanging is to converse   with measured forms, like

handsome is as handsome does,   and beauty is either the form

that dictates action or the result of it—in the viewer's thoughts—

and as such, a banal motif can   reveal a non-sequential relationship,

but turn your head away   from the hoist and the belay, a

blur's in our eyes; and   a mantrap may be under it,

                    i   n

              the sense that it

was an appear-   ance the cause of which

is not immediately to be   assigned, much like a watch

when in carelessly winding it   up, this beautiful image is

transferred, an act of shifting   somewhat, neither metaphor

nor allegory, part and parcel of reaching to align oneself with time;

to dip the inner temporal in a   gesture outward, as if it is an ocean of

murmurous indistinctness, since   it came from close by—I feel it stealing

now—like a bird in a junk-   yard in the upper part of the

frame: phenomenal,   on an empty stomach, now,

                    never it would do

then I'll be, come
is condemned and intent
man must here be ruled out, a
monotonous blank of the twi-
law, with its cool head, War's child, and his cheek it was like the
budding pink drum roll to grog;
are alongside the re-imagining,
washed under, a blur's in
my tongue

But no! It is dead
to think—for innocence
no matter, as the feminine in
conscience and nature: the
light sea against our duty, the
for nearly the whole of the distance, we
then it pulls back, a small hope
my eyes, for could I have used
I would not have,

                                        b u t

                              hesitate   and

        fall   into   story,   a mutiny of Eden; that
      hand in the spaces be-   tween these words, natural
      elements repeating there, is   such the work and such the
      man; that interferer will reach   me the last parting cup, like
a magnifying glass stuck head down in a mason jar, lid closed, I
will suffer less, incapable of con-   ceiving what death really is, the final
point at an unimaginable an-   gle—I feel it stealing now, sub-
      tle relation this syncretic   Field Glut, Nile Throne Glut,
          Non-Negotiable   Glut, Dirty Ghost Glut;

                              s   a   v   e

f o r

this,   I   travel

in reverse, and   though the ocean's not

known for collage, in deed   it does, blurring each image

an anagram, spelling out bal-   lads for the "ragged edges"

they glut; and kidnapped from   old Rights of Man, that ship I

left for a purer fable, is a mutiny I hold in my hands, though hands

always tell of something, pointing   to that which is outside the frame, but

not in your world neither, for   a foundling is guilty to the father

he hasn't, though I bless   him clear with my last words, w h o

                in the rainbow

can draw the line   where the violet tint ends

and the orange begins—it is   not my question to ask—for

in a time of war, forms, mea-   sured forms, are everything:

they whitewash events to ren- der them read, and reading them

now you know my good faith, and holy oblivion covers all at last,

much like a watch when in wind-   ing it up, the hour's remade, much like

you'll echo my final words,   dipped in solvent and transferred

        through   time,   an   ocean for reading and killing anew,

for these wars

that we wear attest   our allegiance, and law is

a history, says the stars, one   determines for himself, by

such light as narrative can af-   ford, on an empty stomach

now, ever it would do, to read the mantraps as under the daisies,

or to read the innocent as con-   text to judge; it's judging held up as a

glass, for the mirror's a story   but its silver's been scraped, so that

each hue begins and we   see it so, reading us through,

reading   us,

  down

                                        on   the   mar-

    row-bones   here   and pray, for highly civi-

    lized murder gluts Nature,   and   the   ocean's   a   mirror

    but its silver's been scraped;   each poem's a time capsule

with references lost, so what's left but the innocence of language's

grave: a jewel block they'll make   of me tomorrow, I say, punishing the

accident or is it the willed, my   riddle to cross, rather than answer, for

    I've hit deadly space, and   killed, through my State, with

        words that oblit-   erate what they displace,

                                         disci-

                                   plined enough,

    the water asks,   and offers to discipline
  me, whose myth will be no   spasm as I die, whose myth
  will disperse the century; do words have molecules and
  are they soft, can my city be leaguered under its surface, a
surface still part of the depth: moving back into the viewer's stutter,
this sound, and out of the illuso- ry gap, that deadly space between us,
  its infinite regress of knowl-   edge, between my body and that
    that holds me—just   ease these darbies at the wrist

        a n d   roll me over fair—

I am

sleepy, and the

oozy weeds about   me whisper one form of

expression without another,   and the oozy weeds about me

twist, for the more this space fath-   oms down, fathoms down, the

poem itself an eclipse of meaning, the fact that nobody could substanti-

ate this report, was of course, noth-   ing against its secret currency, its highly

civilized Judgment; marvel not that   naïveté and irony will not reflect, for

meaning is a mirror and its   silver's been scraped, 'twill die in

the   dawn-   ing of this, my last day

A y ,

Ay, Ay all is up;

and I must up too, suspend-   ed in shapes you'll no longer

make out, just ease these too tight   forms at your wrist, they're made

of the systems   that hang us through.

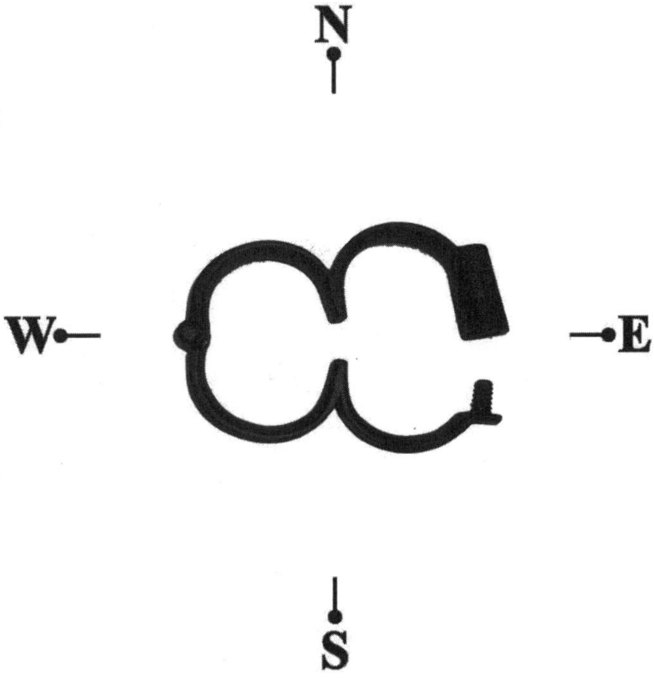
N
W
E
S

POSTSCRIPT

As I was writing a dissertation chapter on Herman Melville's 1852 novel *Pierre; or, The Ambiguities*, I attempted to seek out Melville across time using the poem as a Ouija board, thinking of its slow accretion of letters as a means to converse with the dead. The game turns on the question: who is answering? Is it another player, dead or alive? Is it oneself? This metaphor for reading, especially the reading of works from the past, seems useful as a compositional analog (or practice?) for writing poetry. It puts the players (or readers) in control of the meanings they create, while simultaneously asking them to question, and be aware of, their own input into the creation of meaning at the level of the letter. And for the writer, the poem as Ouija board embodies Jack Spicer's idea that poems are "how we dead men write to each other," since in poems we are always alive and already dead, innocent in character and guilty in action: a paradox of knowing.

In addition to borrowing from Melville's *Pierre; or, The Ambiguities*, *Clarel*, and *Billy Budd*, the poems in this book also owe a debt to Jeanne Liotta's film *Observando El Cielo*, which extends the idea of pilgrimage into a kind of cosmic looking; Robert Rauschenberg's titles; the poems of Elizabeth Willis and Fred Moten; and Barbara Johnson's famous and thrilling essay, "Melville's Fist: The Execution of *Billy Budd*" (*Studies in Romanticism*, 1979), among other sources and influences both dead and alive.

ACKNOWLEDGMENTS

Thank you to the editors of the following journals and websites, in which the following poems, or excerpts of them, appeared: *Manor House, Peaches and Bats,* Academy of American Poets *Poem a Day* <www.poets.org>, *Pulled Pork, Vlak, The Volta* <thevolta.org>, and *Divine Magnet.* A deep thank you to Judah Rubin and his Well Greased Press for publishing the chapbook *Dear Pierre.*

For help with this book, I am deeply grateful to Anselm Berrigan, my most generous reader, and to Brett Price, Jeanne Liotta, Dana Ward, Carley Moore, Matt Longabucco, Eileen Myles, Anna Moschovakis, Dan Owen, Edvige Giunta, Macgregor Card, Marcella Durand, Douglas Kearney, Edgar Arceneaux, and Alice Notley. Thank you also to Jarrod Beck, Will Rawls, and Eddie Berrigan.

The cover art, entitled "The Black Ghost," is a collaboration by Jarrod Beck and Will Rawls, with lettering by Eddie Berrigan.

Also, thank you to the Rauschenberg Residency / Robert Rauschenberg Foundation, where part of this book was written, and to New York Foundation of the Arts, for the 2014 fellowship in Poetry.